Amazing Animals
Birds

Please visit our Web site, www.garethstevens.com. For a free color catalog of all our high-quality books, call toll free 1-800-542-2595 or fax 1-877-542-2596.

Library of Congress Cataloging-in-Publication Data

Barnard, Edward S.
 Birds / Edward S. Barnard.
    p. cm. — (Amazing animals)
 Includes index.
 ISBN 978-1-4339-4008-8 (pbk.)
 ISBN 978-1-4339-4009-5 (6-pack)
 ISBN 978-1-4339-4007-1 (library binding)
 1. Birds—Juvenile literature. I. Title.
 QL676.2.B355 2010
 598—dc22
                                        2010000490

This edition first published in 2011 by
Gareth Stevens Publishing
111 East 14th Street, Suite 349
New York, NY 10003

Editor: Greg Roza
Designer: Christopher Logan

Photo credits: Cover, back cover, pp. 18–19, 20–21, 26–27, 32–33, 34–35, 37 (bottom), 41 (pelican) Shutterstock.com; pp. 1, 3 © Dreamstime.com/Tzeroung Tan; pp. 4–5 © iStockphoto.com/Hanis; pp. 6–7 © iStockphoto.com/Andrew Howe; pp. 8–9, 8 (top left), 9 (bottom), 10–11, 10 (bottom left), 12–13, 13 (bottom), 18 (bottom left), 19 (top center), 28 (pigeon) © Edward S. Barnard; pp. 14–15 © iStockphoto.com/Emory Moody; pp. 16–17, 22 (bottom left), 34–35 © Corbis; p. 17 (bones) © Dreamstime.com/Tommounsey; pp. 21 (top), 27 (bottom) © iStockphoto.com/Mr. Jamsey; p. 21 (middle) © iStockphoto.com/EcoPic; p. 21 (bottom) © iStockphoto.com/han36; pp. 22–23, 44–45 © IT Stock; pp. 24–25 © iStockphoto.com/Charlie Bishop; p. 28 (quelea) © Dreamstime.com/Johannes Gerhardus Swanepoel; pp. 28–29 © iStockphoto.com/Qualisule; pp. 30–31, 42–43 © iStockphoto.com/Bird Images; p. 32 (bottom) © iStockphoto.com/Yourmap; p. 33 (bottom) © iStockphoto.com/Missing35mm; p. 34 (bottom) Photodisc/Getty Images; pp. 36–37 © iStockphoto.com/Jjacob; pp. 38–39 © Dreamstime.com/Sara Robinson; pp. 40–41 © iStockphoto.com/Joe Gough; p. 41 (sandpipers) © iStockphoto.com/DHuss; p. 42 (bottom) © Dreamstime.com/Photoshow; p. 46 Wikimedia Commons.

Printed in the United States of America

CPSIA compliance information: Batch #CS10GS: For further information contact Gareth Stevens, New York, New York at 1-800-542-2595.

Amazing Animals
Birds

By Edward S. Barnard

Gareth Stevens
Publishing

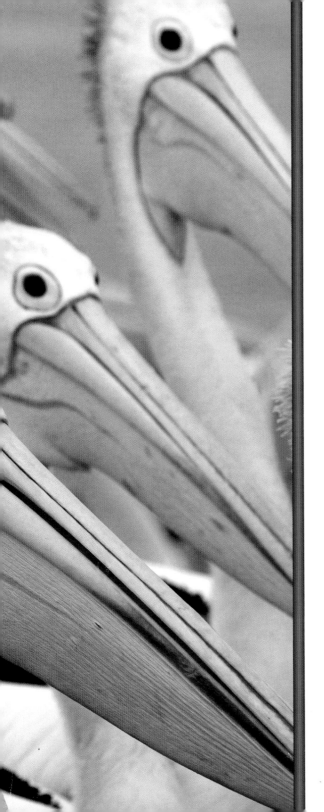

Contents

Chapter 1

A Tale of Terns

Terns Take Turns

A female common tern lays two or three eggs in late May. Then she and her mate take turns sitting on the eggs until they hatch 23 days later.

A male common tern comes in for a landing near his nesting mate. The pair are living on an island with thousands of other tern pairs.

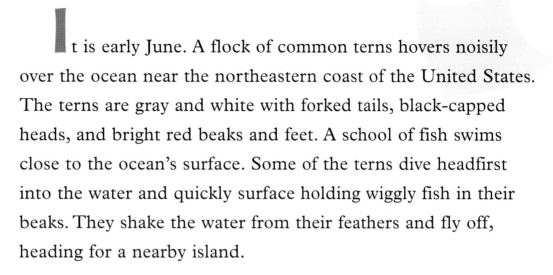

It is early June. A flock of common terns hovers noisily over the ocean near the northeastern coast of the United States. The terns are gray and white with forked tails, black-capped heads, and bright red beaks and feet. A school of fish swims close to the ocean's surface. Some of the terns dive headfirst into the water and quickly surface holding wiggly fish in their beaks. They shake the water from their feathers and fly off, heading for a nearby island.

A male tern lands near a female sitting on a nest in a hollow place on the ground. She has two tan, speckled eggs underneath her. She is hungry and quickly swallows the fish her mate offers as they exchange places on the nest.

Dinnertime!

Most of the time, common terns catch fish for their young. But tern parents also feed their little ones insects, shrimp, and small crabs.

Soon it is mid-June. Two tiny, fluffy baby birds hatch from the eggs. The female tern squats over the chicks, shading them from the hot sun. The male tern flies in from the ocean with a fish for one of the chicks. The fish is almost as big as the chick! It dangles from the chick's beak for a minute or so but finally disappears. Both parents look for food and feed the chicks. The male tern brings them more fish than the female does.

The tern colony is a noisy place during the day. Hundreds of terns call out *ter-arr* and make rapid *kip-kip-kip* sounds as they swoop and circle in the sky. Sometimes a few gulls fly close to the island, hoping to carry off a tern chick or two. Then hundreds of shrieking terns angrily take to the air and chase the gulls away.

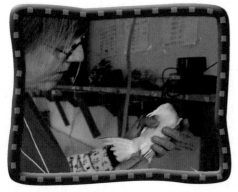

Weighed and Measured

Scientists study terns on Great Gull Island, near New York City. They weigh the birds, measure their beaks, and put tiny numbered bands on their legs. When a banded bird is caught again, sometimes years later in another place, the band will show scientists where the bird came from.

A newly born common tern chick grows fast. After a week, it may weigh three times as much as it did when it hatched.

The young common tern, standing next to a parent, is about 24 days old. Its wing feathers are not fully grown.

As the tern chicks grow, new and larger feathers replace their down, or tiny, fluffy feathers. Gray and brown feathers **sprout** on their wings. Black feathers cover their heads.

Once the young terns grow wing feathers, they try to fly. By the time they are 3 or 4 weeks old, they take to the air for short flights. Their parents still bring them fish, sometimes feeding them in midair. In another week or two, the young terns will fly longer distances to catch their own fish. Their parents will stop feeding them, and they will then take care of themselves.

As summer ends, thousands of young terns gather in flocks. Soon they will leave the island and fly more than 4,000 miles (6,400 km) to South America. They will live along the coast of Brazil or Argentina for 2 years and then return to the island where they were born to raise their own families.

Ready to Take Off

This young tern is learning to fly. Scientists on Great Gull Island call birds at this stage "Orvilles," after Orville Wright, one of the inventors of the airplane.

Chapter 2
The Body of a Bird

The male peafowl, also called a peacock, fans out his **iridescent** feathers to impress peahens, the females. Peahens have plainer, shorter feathers.

Feathers and Bones

Birds are the only animals with feathers. Feathers help them maintain their body heat. Birds are **warm-blooded**, which means their body temperature always stays the same. Feathers also make it possible for birds to fly. Without wing and tail feathers, birds couldn't get off the ground. In addition, feathers give birds color— for **camouflage** and for attracting mates.

It is believed that birds are **descended** from dinosaurs and their feathers developed from scales. In fact, birds still have scales on their legs. Birds have very lightweight bones, which are usually hollow. A bird's bones can actually be lighter than all of its feathers.

Special Bones

A bird that is a strong flier or swimmer has a large breastbone. The big muscles powering the bird's wings attach to the breastbone.

A bird has more bones in its neck than a human does. This allows the bird to turn its head to face backward.

Wings and Feet

Every bird has wings—even birds that can't fly, such as penguins. A bird's wing is curved. This curved shape helps to give the wing **lift**. As a bird flaps its wings, its feathers twist to let air through on the upstroke and flatten to catch more air on the downstroke.

The shape of a bird's wing is different depending on the bird's way of life. The fastest bird is the peregrine falcon. Its swept-back, streamlined wings allow it to dive for prey at more than 175 miles (280 km) per hour! Vultures have broad, rounded wings that let them hover in the air as they scan the ground below for food. Birds that don't fly much, such as pheasants, have short, stubby wings.

Feet with a Difference

Feet tell a lot about how birds live. Many waterbirds that swim have webbed feet. Most **perching birds** have one toe that points backward to help them grasp tree branches and hold tight. Eagles have muscular toes and sharp **talons** for clutching prey.

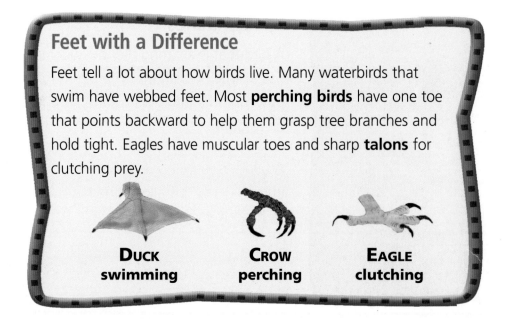

DUCK
swimming

CROW
perching

EAGLE
clutching

Flying Lesson

LOW PRESSURE

HIGH PRESSURE

LIFT ↑

The pressure of air flowing under a bird's wings is greater than the pressure of air above them. The pressure from below pushes (lifts) the wings up.

As a great egret flaps its wings, the wing feathers fan out to catch the air. The bird's long legs and long, thin toes allow it to wade in water and walk on mud.

Toucans, birds of the tropical rain forests, have large but lightweight beaks. The beaks are perfect for picking fruits, attracting mates, and fighting with rivals.

Beaks and Eyes

Birds don't have teeth. Instead, they have bony beaks, which are also called bills. The shape of a bird's beak usually depends on what the bird eats. Woodpeckers have sharp beaks for digging holes into trees to reach burrowing insects. Spoonbills have long, flattened bills that they swing slowly back and forth in water to strain out tiny animals and plants.

woodpecker

spoonbill

Some birds have eyes on the sides of their heads, allowing them to see **predators** approaching from almost any direction. The eyes of **birds of prey** face forward. This helps them judge distances. Some birds can see detail and color better than humans. Golden eagles can spot hares that are 1 mile (1.6 km) away!

Owl

Big Bird and Little Bird

Like other birds, an ostrich has feathers, wings, a beak, and two legs. The female lays eggs. Unlike most other birds, however, ostriches can't fly. That is because of their size. Ostriches are the world's heaviest, tallest, and fastest-running birds. They can weigh 350 pounds (160 kg). They can have a height of 9 feet (2.7 m)—taller than the tallest basketball player! They can run as fast as a racehorse. They lay the world's heaviest eggs—each one weighs as much as 24 chicken eggs!

The smallest bird is the bee hummingbird of Cuba. It is only 2.5 inches (6.4 cm) long—about the length of an adult's little finger. It weighs less than a penny and lays pea-sized eggs.

Sweet Snack

Hummingbirds dine on insects and the nectar, or sweet liquid, in flowers. They eat more than their weight in food every day. They are the only birds that can hover for long periods and fly backward or straight up!

Ostriches live in groups of 100 or more. They can't fly, but they wave their wings to attract mates and use them for balance when they run.

Chapter 3
Perching Birds

The cardinal probably deserves the title of America's most popular songbird. Seven states have named it their official state bird! Unlike many other songbirds, it does not fly south for the winter.

Biggest Bird Group

There are over 9,500 different kinds, or **species**, of birds in the world. More than half belong to a group called perching birds. These birds have three toes facing forward and one pointing backward. When a perching bird begins to lean backward, its feet tighten their grip. This makes it possible for the bird to easily cling to twigs, reeds, and power lines—even when it is asleep!

Some perching birds are songbirds. They have special throat muscles that are used for singing. Many songbirds, such as sparrows and warblers, make sounds that are pleasant for us to listen to. Songbirds sing to attract mates and to keep rivals out of their nesting grounds. They also use songs to signal danger and tell others about new feeding places. Chicks use songs to tell parents they are hungry.

Fewer Bluebirds

Like the cardinal, the bluebird is a beautiful and popular songbird, but its numbers are decreasing. Starlings and house sparrows compete with it for its favorite nesting spots—empty holes in old trees and fence posts.

Billions of Birds

Perching birds are the most plentiful birds on the planet. There are almost a half billion starlings and house sparrows in the United States. Pigeons live in nearly every major city in the world.

pigeon

Every spring, red-winged blackbirds nest in North American farmlands, marshes, and lakeshores. Flying in large flocks, the males arrive first and announce their territories with repeated calls. A few days later, the females fly in. After the pairs raise their young, they form huge flocks that sometimes number in the millions.

Hungry Hordes

The red-billed quelea of Africa is the world's most numerous species of bird. There are over 1.5 billion of them! When a **horde** of queleas settles on a farm, the birds can cause serious crop damage.

This flock of red-winged blackbirds and yellow-headed blackbirds built their nests in a large marsh. The red-winged blackbirds nested around the edges of the marsh, and the yellow-heads nested in the center.

Chapter 4
Birds of Prey

To cut down on wind resistance, an osprey carries the fish it has just caught headfirst. Barbed pads on the osprey's feet help this bird keep a firm grip on its slippery prey.

Gigantic Nests

This huge osprey nest is built on top of a cactus in California. Ospreys often reuse nests and add new sticks each season. A large osprey nest can weigh 1,000 pounds (450 kg) or more!

Eagles and Hawks

A bird of prey hunts by using its talons to catch fish, mice, rabbits, and other birds. Eagles are large, powerful birds of prey. They have keen eyesight, hooked beaks for tearing flesh, and broad wings for fast flight.

Hawks are medium-sized birds of prey. Some have longer tails and shorter wings than eagles. Other hawks, such as the red-tailed hawk, have long, wide wings. They can soar for hours, seldom flapping their wings.

The osprey lives on every continent in the world except Antarctica. It hunts by diving feet first into water and grabbing fish near the surface.

Fierce Hunter

The golden eagle uses its talons for killing and carrying prey. The talons are much stronger than the hands of a human being.

Hunters of the Night

Most birds of prey hunt in the daytime, but owls usually hunt at night and roost in trees during the day. Before they begin to hunt, owls comb their head feathers with their talons. Then they take off silently on wings edged with extra-soft feathers that muffle sound.

An owl's eyes face forward like ours do, helping them judge distances well. Their eyes are very big compared to the size of their heads. Owls also have excellent hearing and can even pinpoint the exact location of mice under snow.

An owl often perches on a low tree branch or fence post, waiting for an animal to move. Then it swoops down silently with its talons stretched out. Often the owl hits its prey hard enough to stun it before grabbing the creature.

Day Hunter

The snowy owl lives in treeless Arctic regions. Unlike most other owls, it hunts in the daytime. Its white feathers help it blend into its surroundings.

Owls have super night vision. Their eyes are up to 100 times more sensitive to light than ours. They can catch prey in almost total darkness!

The Andean condor of South America is the world's largest bird of prey. Its **wingspan** is about 10.5 feet (3.2 m)! Like other vultures, it has only a few feathers on its head because they would get dirty when it eats.

Vultures

Vultures are birds of prey that feed on dead or dying animals. They don't carry food to their young. They eat the food first, then **disgorge** it directly into the chick's mouth. Many people consider vultures disgusting, but they play a very important role in the web of life. They help get rid of rotting meat that might kill other animals if they were to eat it.

Condors are the largest vultures. Males weigh up to 33 pounds (15 kg). Condors live in the mountains of California and South America. They can soar for hours high in the sky with hardly a flap. When they spot dead animals or other vultures already feeding, they land and rip into the hides of even the toughest **carcasses**.

Lord of the Vultures

The king vulture lives in the rain forests of South America. Other vultures make way for these big, **aggressive** birds.

Chapter 5
Waterbirds

A puffin is one of the few birds that can hold several fish in its beak at once!

Birds of Sea and Shore

Some seabirds, such as gannets and puffins, live out in the open ocean for many months each year. They feed on fish by diving underwater. In the spring and summer, these birds come ashore on islands, where thousands of them nest close together.

pelican

Pelicans stay close to shore most of the time. They have a stretchy pouch under the lower part of their big bill. After diving and scooping up a fish and water, the pelican comes to the surface. The water drains out of the pouch, and the pelican swallows the fish.

Gulls stay along the shore, too. They eat seafood and anything else they can find—insects, dead animals, berries, and even garbage!

Keeping Dry

Sandpipers always stay just ahead of the surf as they run along the seashore. And somehow they know exactly where to stick their bills into the sand to catch worms and small crabs.

Wetland Birds

Lakes, rivers, streams, ponds, and marshes are good places to see birds. Even ponds in city parks are likely to have ducks, geese, and swans. Wet places offer birds water, food, and protection from predators.

Pond ducks usually feed in the water near the shore. They snap up tiny plants floating in the water and tip over headfirst to pull up plants from the pond's muddy bottom. Swans also feed on underwater plants. Geese feed on land, grazing on grass and grain.

Long-legged wading birds—such as cranes, storks, and herons—stand quietly in shallow water waiting for fish or frogs to come within range of their lightning-quick, sharply pointed beaks.

Saved!

Wood ducks were once **endangered** because of hunting and the cutting down of their nesting trees. To help save these ducks, many people put nest boxes around woodland lakes and ponds. Now these beautiful ducks can be seen once again.

For the Birds

Many waterbirds and some of our most beautiful songbirds are in trouble because of changes in their **habitats**. Find out how you can help them by contacting your local Audubon Society.

The great blue heron feeds in shallow water, grabbing or spearing fish, frogs, crayfish, snakes, or anything else moving. It stands 4 feet (1.2 m) tall and has a 7-foot (2.1-m) wingspan.

Glossary

aggressive—showing the tendency to attack or do harm for little reason

bird of prey—a meat-eating bird, such as an eagle, owl, or hawk, that hunts for food. Some birds of prey eat animals that are dying or dead.

camouflage—colors or shapes in animals that help them blend in with their surroundings

carcass—a dead body

descended—connected by blood to a type of animal that lived in the past

disgorge—throw up food that has been swallowed

endangered—a species of animal or plant in danger of dying out

habitat—the natural environment where an animal or plant lives

horde—a large group

iridescent—colorful and shiny

lift—air pressure that pushes a wing upward

perching bird—a bird with three toes facing forward and one backward to grip branches and other resting places

predator—an animal that hunts and eats other animals to survive

species—a group of plants or animals that are the same

sprout—to appear and grow rapidly

talons—sharp claws on a bird of prey

warm-blooded—having a body temperature that stays the same even when the outside temperature changes

wingspan—the distance between wing tips

Birds: Show What You Know

scarlet robin

How much have you learned about birds? Grab a piece of paper and a pencil and write your answers down.

1. How long does it take common tern eggs to hatch?

2. What does "warm-blooded" mean?

3. Name three reasons feathers are important to birds.

4. What is the fastest bird?

5. What is the largest bird?

6. What is the smallest bird?

7. How many species of birds are there in the world?

8. Why do songbirds sing?

9. Why do most birds of prey have hooked beaks?

10. What waterbird tips over headfirst to pull up plants from the bottom of a pond?

1. 23 days 2. Having a body temperature that stays the same even when the outside temperature changes 3. Feathers keep birds warm, they make it possible for birds to fly, and they give birds color. 4. The peregrine falcon 5. The ostrich 6. The bee hummingbird 7. Over 9,500 8. To attract mates, keep rivals away, signal danger, and tell others about feeding grounds 9. To tear flesh 10. Pond ducks

For More Information

Books

Burnie, David. *Bird*. New York, NY: DK Publishing, Inc., 2008.

Choiniere, Joseph, and Claire Mowbray Golding. *What's That Bird? Getting to Know the Birds Around You, Coast to Coast*. North Adams, MA: Storey Publishing, 2005.

Winner, Cherie. *Everything Bird: What Kids Really Want to Know About Birds*. Minnetonka, MN: NorthWord, 2007.

Web Sites

Birds.com
www.birds.com
Learn all about birds, including how to identify them, observe them, and even how to care for injured birds.

The National Audubon Society
www.audubon.org
Find information about birds and what you can do to keep them and their habitats safe.

Index